THE
EXERCISE
OF OUR
SPIRIT
FOR THE
RELEASE
OF THE
SPIRIT

WITNESS LEE

Living Stream Ministry
Anaheim, CA • www.lsm.org

First Edition, February 2004.

ISBN 0-7363-2554-9

Published by

Living Stream Ministry
2431 W. La Palma Ave., Anaheim, CA 92801 U.S.A.
P. O. Box 2121, Anaheim, CA 92814 U.S.A.

Printed in the United States of America

04 05 06 07 08 09 10 / 9 8 7 6 5 4 3 2 1

CONTENTS

PREFACE

This book is composed of four messages given by Brother Witness Lee on October 11-13, 1963 in New York City. These messages were not reviewed by the speaker.

Chapter One

OUR COOPERATION WITH THE SPIRIT FOR THE RELEASE OF THE SPIRIT

Scripture Reading: Rom. 8:26-27; Jude 20; 2 Cor. 3:17

In these messages we would like to fellowship regarding the release of the Spirit. We must realize that the relationship between God and us is a relationship in the spirit because the Spirit of God dwells in our spirit, works together with our spirit, and is even joined and mingled together with our spirit. Romans 8:16 says that the Holy Spirit witnesses with our spirit, and 1 Corinthians 6:17 tells us that we are one spirit with the Lord. These verses prove that the divine Spirit and our human spirit have been mingled together to be one spirit.

COOPERATING WITH THE HOLY SPIRIT

The Spirit in our spirit is constantly moving, working, and acting in us in a positive way. First John 2:27 says that the anointing which we have received from the Lord abides in us. This verse does not use the word *ointment* but the word *anointing*, which implies the movement or application of the ointment. The ointment is the Spirit, and the anointing is the action or movement of the Spirit. Thus, this verse proves that the Holy Spirit, who is within us today as the ointment, is constantly moving, working, and acting in us in a positive way. This is similar to the electricity in a house, which continually circulates throughout the house as a current. If there is no current, practically speaking there is no electricity. Thus, in order for there to be a current of electricity in the house, the electricity must constantly move, circulate, and flow throughout the house. Likewise, the Holy Spirit within us is always moving.

However, the problem today is that much of the time we limit, frustrate, and hinder the moving, working, and acting of the Spirit. The problem is not that the Spirit is not working in us. On the contrary, the Spirit is always working. The problem is that we do not cooperate with the Spirit enough. We may illustrate this by using the example of marriage. A marriage is a union of two persons as one, but if the wife never cooperates whenever her husband acts, the husband can do nothing. This is like our relationship with the Lord. The Lord has mingled Himself with us and is now working within us, but we do not cooperate with Him that much. We often pray for the Lord to work, saying, "Lord, we are waiting for You to work," but we do not realize that He is waiting for us to cooperate with Him. He may be saying to us, "I have been waiting a long time for you to cooperate." The problem is not with the Lord but with us. This basic principle of the need for our cooperation must be very clear to us.

We can confirm this principle by our experience. When we do not exercise our spirit, we choke off the Spirit. This is like closing the flue in a fireplace. When we close the flue and choke off the source of air, there is no draft or air current for the fire to burn. Many times we choke off the moving, anointing, and burning of the Spirit in a similar way. We do not cooperate with the Spirit and instead quench the fire of the Spirit (cf. 1 Thes. 5:19; 2 Tim. 1:6).

The Spirit is waiting for an opportunity to burn. If we would simply give the Spirit a chance to burn, He would burn. Thus, the responsibility is on us. If we wanted to start a fire, it would be ridiculous for us to pray to the fire, saying, "Fire, please burn." If the fire could speak, it would answer, saying, "You must first cooperate with me. You must apply me to something so that I can burn." There is no need to pray to the fire. The fire is ready and waiting for a chance to burn, and if we would simply cooperate by opening the flue, bringing some wood, and adding some oil, the fire would burn. It is the same with the Spirit. In the past I saw many people pray, "Lord, fill us with the Holy Spirit. We are waiting for the outpouring of Pentecost." Most of the time this kind of prayer did not work. However, we know by experience that whenever we cooperate with the Holy Spirit, the Spirit is released.

We must be clear that the problem regarding the filling or working of the Holy Spirit is not a problem with the Holy Spirit. Rather, the problem is with us. If we do not cooperate with the Spirit or are not willing or ready, the Spirit can do nothing. All He can do is wait until we are willing and ready.

PRAYING ACCORDING TO THE ANOINTING

Also, if we want to be ready and willing for the filling of the Spirit, we must pray (Acts 1:14). When we pray for this matter, we must forget about our circumstances, our memories, and all the thoughts in our mind. Instead, we must take care of the sense, feeling, or consciousness in the innermost part of our being. This sense is the anointing of the Holy Spirit within us (1 John 2:20, 27). When we pray for this matter, we must take care of this feeling and utter what we sense in our innermost part. We must not be bothered by our needs or circumstances. Instead, we must go to the Lord and take care of the feeling in the innermost part of our being.

For instance, suppose there is a brother whose wife is seriously ill. If you were this brother, and you were going to the Lord to pray, could you forget about your wife's illness? This would not be easy. Surely your wife's illness would be on your mind. However, if you want to learn how to pray, you must exercise to forget about everything when you go to the Lord. Even if your wife is seriously ill, you must forget about that and take care of the innermost sense. You must not pray according to your circumstances, needs, memory, or what others have requested; rather, you must pray according to what you sense in your innermost being.

When you go to the Lord in this way, even though you may be unable to forget your wife's illness, you may have a deep sense to pray concerning something else. You may kneel down and cry, "Lord, I am so sinful. Lord, I have been wrong with my wife." You will simply forget about your wife's illness and utter what is within the innermost part of your being. By praying in this way, you exercise your spirit to release the

Spirit who is in your spirit. It is even possible that your wife will be healed by this kind of prayer. I am not saying that if your wife is ill that you should not pray for her to be healed. Rather, I am saying that when you go to the Lord, you must take care of the deep sense within you. You must utter what is in the innermost part of your being.

If we go to the Lord to pray in this way, the first thing the Holy Spirit will do is to purge and purify us. If we forget about our circumstances, the outward requests from others, and even our own thoughts and simply pray according to our inner sense, the Holy Spirit will purge and purify us. We may tell the Lord, "Lord, I am so sinful and dirty in many matters. My motives are wrong, and my intentions are not pure. I am always seeking something for myself." This is real prayer. If we pray in this way, we may be assured that we are in the spirit. The more we pray according to our innermost feeling, the more we will be in the spirit and the more the Spirit will fill us. Ultimately, we will be filled with the Spirit.

THE EXERCISE OF OUR SPIRIT

Our problem today is not with teaching or knowledge but with the exercise of our spirit. How often during the day do we exercise our spirit to release the Holy Spirit? I am afraid that a number of us may not even know how to exercise our spirit. We know how to exercise our arms and legs, but we do not know how to exercise and use our spirit. The best way to exercise our legs and feet is to walk or run, and the best way to exercise our spirit is to pray. However, when we pray, we often exercise our mind instead of exercising our spirit. Thus, in order to exercise our spirit, we must forget all our thoughts and outward circumstances and take care of our inner sense.

Sometimes while we pray, we simultaneously consider and think about various matters in our mind. Outwardly we may be praying, but inwardly we are absolutely in our mind and not in our spirit. This is not real prayer; rather, it is somewhat artificial. An artificial prayer is one in which we do not care for the inner sense and simply pray according to the considerations and thoughts in our mind. Real prayer is when we do not care about our circumstances or about who is around us and simply utter what is in our spirit, praying from our innermost part. Many times when others are praying, we have the sense that their prayers are from the mind and not the spirit. We do not sense the anointing within; there is no echo within us. However, sometimes we hear someone pray, and there is an anointing or response within us. That kind of prayer touches our innermost being because it is from the spirit, not the mind.

We must learn to pray real prayers, prayers that are uttered from our innermost part. Some may say that they do not have any feeling in their innermost part or that they do not sense the moving or inspiration of the Holy Spirit. This may be true, but this does not mean that we should wait for the inspiration of the Spirit. When we want to start a car, we do not wait for the car to start itself. We simply start the car ourselves. In the same sense, we should not wait for the Spirit to inspire us. The Spirit, like the car, is waiting for us. It is our responsibility to exercise our spirit to release the Spirit.

THE RELEASE OF THE SPIRIT IN THE MEETINGS

If we exercise and release our spirit, the Spirit in our spirit will be released. However, in order to release our spirit, we must open ourselves. Many times we are closed because of our emotions. Perhaps we may have trouble with our spouse, or we may receive some bad news during the day that makes us unhappy. Thus, when we come to the meeting, we come depressed and suppressed. We come to the meeting with our spirit bound by our emotions and become a burden to the meeting. If all the brothers came to the meeting with such a spirit, the atmosphere of the meeting would be very heavy, and no one would want to stay in the meeting. Thus, we must learn to allow our emotions to be broken, to forget about our emotions. We must learn to go along not with our emotions but to go along with our spirit. If we allow our emotions to be broken and learn to release our spirit, the Spirit in our spirit will automatically be released.

This does not mean that we must condemn our emotions. Actually, the more spiritual a person is, the more emotional he will be. The Spirit cannot fill someone who is emotionless.

Thus, you should not be afraid of being emotional. However, it is wrong to be emotional simply in yourself. To be emotional in the spirit is right. This word may seem quite contradictory; on the one hand, we must learn to deny our emotions, and on the other hand, we must learn how to be emotional. However, I believe we can understand this word.

Some people are bound not by their emotions but by their mind. When they come to the meetings, they come with many thoughts and considerations, and these thoughts and considerations put their spirit in bondage. Thus, they must be broken so that they would know how to exercise the spirit and that the Spirit within them would be released. Then there would be a current, a flow, that would refresh, strengthen, and renew others and that would bring life into the meeting. If a few saints came to the meeting with a released spirit, denying their mind, emotion, and will and exercising their spirit, the rest of the saints would be encouraged to also release their spirit.

Our meetings need to be living and full of the moving, burning, and flowing of the Holy Spirit. This kind of meeting will meet many people's needs. Some of us may despise the brothers and sisters who do not come to the meetings. Of course, it is not proper for these saints to neglect the meetings, but we should not despise them. Rather, we must ask why they are not coming to the meetings and also consider what the condition of our meetings is. If our meetings are not living, burning, refreshing, satisfying, and supplying, the saints who are cold or backslidden will not come because they cannot be helped in such meetings. However, if the meetings are burning, living, and refreshing, people will be attracted, and the people who come will receive the help that they need.

The vitality of the meetings depends on the exercise of the spirit. To have a living meeting we all must learn how to exercise our spirit. When we come to the meeting, we should be like the members of a basketball team; we should come not to sit around but to exercise and to pass the ball. However, many times when we come to the meetings, we merely sit, listen, watch, and criticize inwardly. This kind of attitude brings in death. Instead, our attitude should be, "I came to the meeting to exercise my spirit. I do not care whether or not others come. I came here to practice playing ball." We should all exercise our spirit, and we should follow and cooperate with one another, just like the players on a team. This will release the Spirit, release others, and become a great help to everyone.

Our thought is that in the meetings we must advise people, admonish them, and warn them. However, none of this works unless the Holy Spirit is moving. A little moving of the Spirit in the meetings will subdue people, convince them, bring them through their situations, and settle and solve their problems. In a sense, we do not need teachings and knowledge. Today we Christians have much knowledge but not much reality. For instance, we know that we must love others, yet we do not truly love others. This is because we are not in the current of the Spirit and do not give the Spirit a chance to move in us. What we need is the current, the moving, and the flowing of the Spirit through us and from within us. Teachings are useful but only when they are given in the flow and current of the Holy Spirit. Without the flow of the Holy Spirit, teachings are dead and useless.

There is no need to be formal in the meetings. Formality in the meetings brings in death and kills the meetings. When our meetings are too formal, those who come to our meetings sense that something is binding them. Sometimes when the saints come to the meeting early, they wait, looking at the clock until one of the responsible brothers stands up to formally begin the meeting. However, if we all came in with a released spirit, denying our mind, emotion, and will, we would begin to pray regardless of what time it was. We would simply pray to release our spirit, and the Holy Spirit would be released. If more saints came to the meeting, their spirits would also be released, and they would be burned because there would already be something burning in the meeting. Perhaps there would not even be the need for someone to announce a hymn or share a message. I am not saying that we should be without order. There must be a proper order, but this does not mean that we must be formal. To be proper is one thing, and to be formal is another. If we would simply release our spirit and give the Holy Spirit the opportunity to be released, the Spirit would have the freedom and the liberty in the meeting, and the spirits of the saints would be strengthened, refreshed, renewed, nourished, and satisfied.

This is what is on my heart. Our meetings need the release of the Spirit. We must break through all the barriers and bonds of our emotions, our mind, our will, and our forms. We must all exercise our spirit to overcome and conquer this kind of situation. When we come to the meetings, we should simply release our spirit. If the Spirit is released in our meetings, our meetings will always be rich. People will be attracted and drawn to the meetings, and the size of the meetings will constantly increase. We each must bear the burden and responsibility for this matter. It is not the responsibility of any one person but of everyone. If we do not take up this responsibility, it is meaningless for us to come together, because the purpose of our coming together is to exercise our spirit that the Spirit would be released and that the Lord would be exalted, magnified, exhibited, and glorified. When the Spirit is bound and suppressed, the Lord is very much limited and hindered. The devil, God's enemy, is the source of death, and his wish and desire is to bring death into the meetings. When there is death in the meetings, he is happy. Therefore, we must fight the battle against the devil. We must tell the Lord, "Lord, we do not agree with death in the meetings. We do not agree that death would be so prevailing in our meetings." We must fight the battle with the help of the Spirit.

QUESTIONS AND ANSWERS

Question: Should we use our mind to think before we begin to pray?

Answer: Many times when we go to the Lord, we are thinking. However, there is no need to think before we go to the Lord and pray. When we go to the Lord, we must forget about everything and simply go to Him to contact and deal with Him in a real way. We must learn to know nothing except that we are contacting the Lord in the spirit. Then when we come to the meetings, we must be active, positive, and living, and our spirit must be released. When our spirit is released, the Holy Spirit within us will automatically be released, and there will be a current flowing in the meeting. This will be a great help to all those in the meeting. This is what a Christian meeting must be like.

Question: How is the filling of the Holy Spirit that you are speaking of different from what people experience in the Pentecostal movement?

Answer: This matter is absolutely different from the experience in the Pentecostal movement. People in the Pentecostal movement do not actually care about the Holy Spirit. Instead, they are concerned with manufacturing and creating a certain kind of atmosphere in their meetings, which is wrong. Thus, we should not justify the Pentecostal way of meeting. However, neither should we justify the so-called fundamental meetings, which are utterly dead. We should not be like those who criticize the Pentecostal movement yet do not say anything to condemn the condition of the fundamental meetings. The Pentecostal meetings are too much to one extreme, and the fundamental meetings are too much to the other extreme. Many fundamental meetings are dead; there is hardly anything in them but death. We should not follow that way of meeting, nor should we pick up the Pentecostal way of meeting.

In God's eyes, death is much more defiling than sin. There are many types in the Old Testament that prove this (Lev. 11:39; 17:15; Num. 19:11, 13). Whenever someone in the Old Testament touched something that was dead, he had to be kept away from the sanctuary of the Lord for a certain number of days. However, although death is more defiling than sin, we are more sensitive to sin than to death. When we commit a sin, we immediately sense that we are wrong, but when we bring death into the meetings, we do not have the same sense. We must realize that God hates death and that death is the last enemy that the Lord must conquer (1 Cor. 15:26).

We do not agree with the Pentecostal way of maneuvering, manufacturing, and creating an atmosphere in a natural way. However, we must condemn even more the deadness of the fundamental way of meeting. We do not want to go along with either of these ways. Rather, we want to go along with the

Holy Spirit. The Holy Spirit is living, moving, and acting all the time. Thus, when we come to the meeting, we must exercise our spirit to cooperate with Him.

Those in the Pentecostal movement do not take care of others' feelings when they meet together. They simply act according to what they like and do not consider what others may think. This spoils the meeting. When we meet together, we must forget about everything and exercise our spirit. However, when we exercise our spirit and take care of the Holy Spirit, the Holy Spirit will automatically guide us to be considerate of others. This does not mean that we must be silent in the meetings; rather, we must be even more exercised in being considerate of others. We need to be flexible in order to have a proper Christian meeting.

According to the fundamental way of meeting, when we come to the meeting, we must wait for a certain time until we can begin the meeting. This is too formal and traditional. I believe that when the Christians met in the early days of the apostles, they also designated a certain time to meet together, but their meetings were not so formal. I believe that they met in a living way. We do not need to wait until the exact time to begin the meeting. We should simply come and exercise our spirit. If we arrive early, we should not sit and wait for the meeting to begin. Rather, we should exercise our spirit, and then the meeting will start in a spontaneous way, not a formal way. If a meeting is scheduled for eight o'clock, we should arrive fifteen minutes early so that we can exercise our spirit and help others to do the same. Then the meeting will be living and not so formal and dead.

Question: Should we exercise our spirit by praying audibly, or should we exercise our spirit inwardly?

Answer: In the meetings it is better to pray audibly. However, this is not something legal. You may feel that you should pray quietly or silently, or you may feel that you should pray audibly so that others can hear. There should be nothing legal about the way we exercise our spirit.

For many years I have considered and studied the way in which Christians should meet. Several years ago I came to the conclusion that the so-called fundamental way of meeting is absolutely traditional and that the Pentecostal way is absolutely extreme. Thirty years ago I spent much time with those in the Pentecostal movement in order to study their way of meeting. I discovered that they were too extreme and that this hurts and damages the spirit. This way of meeting does not build up.

In the early days of the apostles the Christians did not meet together in the Pentecostal way or the fundamental way but in a flexible way. There were no forms or regulations, yet the meetings were very proper, orderly, living, and free. There was no program, formality, or bondage, and nothing was enforced, such as performing emotional activities. Rather, the believers came together and exercised their spirit. The meetings were very living; everyone had the freedom and liberty to release his or her spirit by singing a hymn, praying, reading a verse, or giving a short testimony. I believe that this is the way the early Christians met and that this is the proper way. If we would practice to meet in this way, our meetings would be uplifted.

The next time we go to a meeting, we should go with the sole purpose of exercising our spirit to worship and exhibit the Lord. We should forget about what time the meeting is supposed to begin and simply exercise our spirit. If we have the sense to pray silently, we should pray silently. If others have the sense to pray audibly, even loudly, we should exercise not to be bothered by that. This is the proper way to meet. We should even be familiar with many of the hymns so that there would be no need for someone to formally announce a hymn. If everyone knows a chorus, someone can lead everyone to sing it at the proper time. This breaks down the barriers and paves the way for the Holy Spirit to go on and have a free way to move. In such a situation everyone is very orderly and well-behaved and yet very living.

We must have a fire burning in our meetings so that when people come, they will be burned and will burn others. We should not have a meeting in which people come together, sit, and look at or listen to something. This is not the building up. We must have a meeting in which the Holy Spirit is released and in which we can be released. This kind of meeting will refresh, renew, release, and satisfy both others and ourselves. This is what the Lord needs, and this is what we need.

When I go to the meetings today, I do not focus on teachings because what I need is something living. When you invite me to a meal, what I care about is not the menu that you give me but the food and drink that you serve. What we should care about is giving others something to eat and drink. Whenever we come together to meet, our meeting should be living, a meeting in which the Holy Spirit moves and is released. This kind of meeting will bring others to the Lord. The unbelievers will be saved, the believers will be edified, nourished, strengthened, delivered, and enlightened, and the Spirit will be released. The Spirit is so rich; He will meet every need, even if there is no formal teaching. We must believe more in what the Holy Spirit can do than in what doctrinal teachings can do.

CHAPTER TWO

EXERCISING OUR SPIRIT
BY PRAISING AND SINGING
IN THE CHURCH MEETINGS

Scripture Reading: Psa. 45:1-15

NEEDING TO BE IN THE SPIRIT
IN ORDER TO OVERFLOW

In this message we would like to see something regarding the flow of the Spirit and the exercise of our spirit in Psalm 45. Psalm 45 is a psalm that praises Christ and speaks of Christ as the King. Verse 1 says, "My heart overflows with a good matter." Overflowing is a matter of our spirit. As Christians we must be constantly overflowing because we have something good to tell people, and this should cause us to praise, sing, and overflow. The people around us, the angels, the demons, and all the created things in this universe should hear us overflowing with a good matter. We all need to be like the psalmist, overflowing with something by speaking forth, singing, and praising.

Verse 1 continues, "I speak what I have composed concerning the King." If we are in the spirit, we will always have something composed concerning the Lord and will always be overflowing. This is not a matter of mere knowledge, teaching, or doctrine but a matter in the spirit and of the spirit. The verse ends by saying, "My tongue is the pen of a ready writer." The composer's pen is his tongue. This indicates that our tongue should always be ready to compose something in praise of the Lord, and the only way we can be ready is by being in the spirit. By exercising our spirit the whole day, we will be like a ready writer. However, if we walk, act, and do things not in the spirit but in the soul or the mind, we will not sing any songs to the Lord. We may sing songs in the meetings when we are with others, but we will not sing songs when we are by ourselves, because such songs can be sung only in the spirit. This is one way we can check whether or not we as Christians are normal.

THE DEATH AND RESURRECTION OF CHRIST SIGNIFIED BY MYRRH AND CASSIA

The next verse speaks of the King, who is Christ the Lord. "You are fairer than the sons of men; / Grace is poured upon Your lips; / Therefore God has blessed You forever" (v. 2). This verse clearly speaks of Christ, who spoke words of grace (Luke 4:22) and is God blessed forever (Rom. 9:5). The first part of Psalm 45:8 says, "All Your garments smell of myrrh and aloes, of cassia." The myrrh and aloes in verse 8 signify the death and burial of Christ. In those days after someone died, his relatives would bury him with myrrh and aloes. After the Lord died on the cross, Nicodemus, a rich man, claimed His body and anointed His body with myrrh and aloes before His burial (John 19:39), indicating that these two spices signify death and burial. Garments in the Scriptures signify a person's deeds or works. Thus, the Lord's righteous deeds and works were full of the sweet-smelling fragrance of His death. Whenever we think of the Lord, His righteousness, and all that He did, we sense the sweetness of His death. This is the sweet smell of myrrh and aloes upon His garments.

Cassia is a kind of wood that produces an oil that is sweet and good for healing. If you want to extract the oil out of the wood, you must "kill" the wood. The wood must suffer death in order for the healing oil to come out from the wood. Thus, cassia signifies Christ in resurrection. The Lord is like the wood; He suffered the killing, and as a result, something came out of Him and into us—the healing Spirit, the Spirit in the Lord's resurrection (John 20:22; cf. Luke 10:34). Whenever we think of the Lord and of His deeds and acts, we automatically sense the sweetness of His death and resurrection.

THE CHURCHES SIGNIFIED BY THE IVORY PALACES

Although this psalm is a psalm of praise of the King, the

second part of the psalm speaks of the queen instead of the King. Verses 8b-13 say, "From palaces of ivory, harpstrings have made You glad / The daughters of kings are among Your most prized; / The queen stands at Your right hand in the gold of Ophir. / Hear, O daughter, and see; and incline your ear; / And forget your people and your father's house; / Thus the King will desire your beauty. / Because He is your Lord, / Worship Him. / And the daughter of Tyre will come with a gift; / The rich among the people will entreat your favor. / The King's daughter is all glorious within the royal abode; / Her garment is a woven work inwrought with gold. / She will be led to the King in embroidered clothing; / The virgins behind her, her companions, / Will be brought to You. / They will be led with rejoicing and exultation; / They will enter the King's palace."

If you read this psalm, you will notice that although it praises the King, it also speaks much about the queen, who is a type of the church. This psalm praises Christ, but it also praises Christ with the church, which was produced after Christ's ascension. Although the psalmist most likely did not know the spiritual significance of what he was writing, the Holy Spirit caused him to write first concerning the death and resurrection of Christ and then concerning the church.

Recently I reviewed a hymn in which the phrase *ivory palaces* from verse 8 was misinterpreted. The hymn implied that the ivory palaces were the heavenly mansions from which the Lord Jesus came to this world of woe. This is not correct, because the king in this psalm is King Solomon, and we know that Solomon is a type of the ascended, glorified, and coming Christ, not the suffering Christ typified by King David. Thus, the writer of the hymn should not have associated King Solomon with the suffering Christ who came down from heaven to this world of woe to suffer. What then is the correct interpretation of the phrase *ivory palaces?* In 1956 we spent much time during a training to study the books of poetry, and we realized something regarding this matter.

The ivory palaces in this psalm are a type of the local churches. Ivory is a kind of bone that has been taken out of a body. In the Scriptures, when a bone is taken out of a body and is separated from it, in a sense the bone passes through death, and after it passes through death, it becomes something. The first mention in the Scriptures of a bone being separated from a body is in Genesis with Adam and Eve (2:21-22). In this example Adam was put to sleep, God opened up his side, and a bone was taken from his side. That bone became Eve, Adam's wife and counterpart, who was a type of the church (Eph. 5:31-32; cf. Gen. 2:24). In the New Testament God did the same thing to Christ. God caused Christ to be put to sleep on the cross and caused His side to be opened, and what came out of Christ's side was blood and water (John 19:34). The water signifies the resurrection life of Christ, and it is by this life that the church came into being. Just as the bone taken out from Adam passed through death and became a wife to Adam, so also the resurrection life of Christ passed through death and became the church, the counterpart of Christ. Thus, the ivory in Psalm 45 signifies the resurrection life of Christ (cf. John 19:36), and the palaces signify the local churches, which come into being through the death and resurrection of Christ.

THE SINGING WITHIN THE CHURCHES

The most significant matter regarding Christ in this psalm is the sweet smell of His death and resurrection, and the most significant matter regarding the church in this psalm is the singing and praising typified by the harpstrings in Psalm 45:8. The early church in the book of Acts is the fulfillment of this psalm. Out of the death and resurrection of Christ came forth many local churches in various places, and from those churches came forth singing and praising to the Lord. This made the Lord glad.

The churches as ivory palaces come out of the death and resurrection of Christ and are in resurrection. Within these dwellings there must be singing all the time, music which makes the Lord glad (Heb. 2:12; Eph. 5:19; Col. 3:16). Thus, we need to sing. It is more difficult to pray than to gossip, and in a sense, it is even more difficult to sing. When we are not in the spirit, it is not easy to sing, but when we are in the spirit, it is easy, and the more we sing, the more we are in the spirit. We must be overflowing, bubbling over, and singing all the time. In our meetings there should be more singing than talking. Because the church is in resurrection, our singing must also be in resurrection. Some people naturally like to sing. However, we should not sing in a natural or emotional way. When we sing, we should not think about the music or try to sing in a musical way. This will kill the singing. Instead, we should sing in a spiritual way. Before the meetings we should learn a new hymn and memorize some choruses or stanzas. Then there will be no need to sing from our hymnals; rather, we can sing from our heart. If we do this, we will see how living, active, and positive our meetings will be. We will be living, and we will be free from the letter and formality.

The right way to exercise our spirit is to pray, but sometimes singing a hymn is even better than praying. If we try singing a hymn in the morning, our spirit will be exercised. The more we sing, the more our spirit will be released and strengthened, and the more our mind will be focused, our will subdued, and our emotions purified. Singing in the proper way will deliver us from our natural mind, emotion, and will. This is the best way to be liberated from the things of the natural life. Our singing is a test of whether or not we are in the spirit. If we are in the spirit, we will constantly be singing. Even while we are driving, we will have a song or a hymn with which to praise the Lord. Our singing and praising are a strong testimony to others that we are Christians.

THE CHURCH BEING IN THE DIVINE NATURE AND FILLED UNTO ALL THE FULLNESS OF GOD

Psalm 45:9 says, "The queen stands at Your right hand in the gold of Ophir." The queen is the church, and the gold is the divine nature of God. Thus, the queen being in the gold of Ophir indicates that the church, which is full of the praises of Christ, is in the divine nature of God (2 Pet. 1:4). Verses 13 and 14 say, "The King's daughter is all glorious within the royal abode; / Her garment is a woven work inwrought with gold. / She will be led to the King in embroidered clothing." The queen is in the gold of Ophir because her clothing is embroidered with gold. This signifies that the divine nature has been wrought into the daily living, walk, conduct, and behavior of the members of the church. In their daily living and walk is the fullness of God. The church as a dwelling place for Christ in His resurrection is in the divine nature and is filled unto all the fullness of God (Eph. 3:19).

The more time I spend with the Lord, the more I feel that it is not the forms, rules, teachings, or doctrines that are important. Rather, what is important is exercising the spirit, realizing the death and resurrection of Christ, practicing the genuine church life, and entering into the fullness of God. We must exercise our spirit which has been mingled with the Holy Spirit so that we may realize the death and resurrection of Christ, having the sweet smell of His resurrection and His golden nature wrought into us. The only way for the whole church to be in the divine nature and full of God is to exercise our spirit, and the best way for us to exercise our spirit is to sing praises to the Lord and to overflow with singing. Psalm 45 is a short psalm, but it is quite meaningful and all-inclusive. In this psalm we have the death of Christ, the resurrection of Christ, the church in resurrection, the singing and praising of the church, and the fullness of God, the expression of God, in the church.

DROPPING THE NEGATIVE THINGS AND EXERCISING OUR SPIRIT TO OVERFLOW AND SING

The saints in the early church had no forms, regulations, teachings, or doctrines. Instead, what they had was the living Christ as the Spirit. Whenever they came together, they were an ivory palace—the issue of the death and resurrection of Christ. They had the inward filling of the Spirit and the outward praising of the Lord and singing to Him from the spirit.

However, during the two thousand years that the church has been on the earth, many negative things that are unnecessary and even troublesome and disturbing have come into the church. Unfortunately, we have been very much influenced by these things. Thus, we must give up all the negative things, including the forms, rules, regulations, teachings, and doctrines. It is not easy to give up and forget about all these things. We have an abundance of many of these negative things and are short of the one positive thing—the praising in our spirit. We must exercise our spirit. Some may be able to give messages or write books on spiritual matters, but they cannot sing a hymn with their spirit. This is not a proper situation. In this situation the mind is too big and active, and the spirit is deadened and dormant. There is almost no activity or functioning in the spirit; rather, all the activity is in the mind. Thus, we must exercise our spirit to sing all the time.

John and Charles Wesley sang every day. If we sang for even half an hour each day, our spirit would be much stronger, and the meetings of the church would be much more living and powerful. The meetings would have an impact and an effect on people because something would be constantly flowing and bubbling in the meetings. As Psalm 45 indicates, we must have these two matters—the overflowing and the singing with the music of the harpstrings. If we are praising, singing, and overflowing all the time, we will realize the death and resurrection of Christ and will be the real ivory palace filled with God. We will have the gold, the divine nature, wrought into us.

We must find a way to release and liberate our spirit and to make our spirit active, living, and strong. We are too strong in the soul and too dormant in our spirit. Too often we pay attention to the body and the soul and neglect the spirit. If we exercise our spirit, the Lord will be liberated because the Lord today is in our spirit as the Spirit. Thus, we must learn to pray and to praise by singing. This will issue in a real deliverance, liberation, and release of our spirit.

CHAPTER THREE

NOT QUENCHING THE SPIRIT

Scripture Reading: 1 Thes. 5:16-19

THE BURNING OF THE SPIRIT
DEPENDING ON THE OPENING OF OUR BEING

The Bible uses many figures to describe the work of the Holy Spirit within us. One figure is that of the living water (John 7:38-39). The Holy Spirit is constantly flowing within us as rivers of living water. Another figure of the Holy Spirit is that of a fire that is constantly burning (Rev. 4:5). We must have both the flowing and the burning of the Spirit in us.

There are several ways to quench a fire, and one way is to cut off its supply of air, the draft. If there is no draft, there is no way for the fire to burn. The burning of the fire depends on the draft. For instance, suppose there is a fire in a stove. If we close off the chimney of the stove and close all the doors and windows, the draft will be choked off, and the fire will be quenched. If we want the fire to burn in a full way, we must open the chimney and the doors and windows. Then the fire can burn freely because there will be a draft, a current of air. Similarly, the burning of the Spirit requires a spiritual draft. If we do not provide the Spirit with the draft, it will be impossible for the Spirit to burn in us.

The fact is that the Holy Spirit is burning within us all the time, but in our experience the Spirit may not always be burning. This is because we often close all the openings of our being and choke off the draft, causing the Spirit to be quenched. This is a very simple yet very vital matter. To have much knowledge but lack the burning of the Spirit within is useless. It is better to be simple, to be on fire, and to let the Holy Spirit burn in us.

THE BURNING OF THE SPIRIT BEING MORE
IMPORTANT THAN KNOWLEDGE

Our problem today is that we lack the burning of the Spirit within. The reason why we Christians are so dead, dormant, weak, cold, and passive is because the fire is not burning within us. We must open our being to let the draft in so that the Spirit can burn in us. We do not need more knowledge. Instead, we should let go of our knowledge and be simple and burning.

When I was young, the Lord was constantly burning in me. Consequently, I was on fire every day. Although I did not have the kind of meetings and help that we have today, the Lord's grace was upon me. There was no need for me to strive or struggle to overcome the worldly things because there was a fire burning within me.

However, after some time I was led to seek the knowledge of the Bible. Day after day for more than five years, I read and studied the Bible merely with my mind. I attended Bible studies and received much knowledge through them. I read many books and papers and learned about matters such as the seventy weeks at the end of Daniel 9. However, the more I studied the Word in this way, the more dead I became. Eventually, the flow of the Spirit stopped, and the burning was quenched. Spiritually, I was dead, and there was no flow or burning within me. With the Lord's help I realized that the way I had taken was wrong. One day I made up my mind and told the Lord, "Lord, I have been wrong. I will give up this kind of studying and instead go to You to contact You and pray to You." From that day on I gave up my studies and stopped going to the study sessions. Instead, every day early in the morning, I went up to the top of a little mountain by my family's house. As I walked up the mountain, I prayed, opening myself to the Lord and giving myself to Him. From the day I began to do this, the flow and the burning of the Spirit within me was recovered; there was something flowing and burning within me again.

As Christians, this fire must be burning within us. Being a Christian is not a matter of merely knowing things. Knowledge apart from the living person of Christ has killed us and is still killing us. The more I have traveled in this country, the more I have discovered that there is too much doctrinal knowledge in Christianity. There are good doctrines, bad doctrines, spiritual doctrines, and other sorts of doctrines, but regardless of whether they are good or bad, mere doctrines and knowledge can damage and kill rather than help. The Bible is not a book of mere doctrine or knowledge; it is the book of the living Word (Heb. 4:12). It is not the tree of knowledge but the tree of life. However, we often take the Bible in the wrong way, taking it as knowledge and not as life (John 5:39-40).

TAKING THE BIBLE IN THE WAY OF LIFE
BY PRAY-READING

How can we take the Bible in the way of life? When we read the Bible, we should exercise our spirit to take in the Word instead of exercising our mind to understand it. We should pray over what we read, understand, and apprehend in order to digest it. After reading the Bible for five minutes, it may be good to pray for ten minutes, praying not concerning various matters but concerning what we have read. We should pray about what we read, pray with what we read, and pray to digest what we read. Then we will realize that the Bible is not a book of knowledge but a book that is full of life and the life supply. The Scriptures clearly tell us that the word that proceeds out from the mouth of God is food to our spirit and is the element that we should receive and by which we should live (Matt. 4:4; John 6:57, 63). However, most of us use the Bible in a wrong way, using it as a book of knowledge to develop our mind. Many Christians have received so much knowledge that it is difficult for them to be inspired by the Word.

We must learn that we need to exercise our spirit and pray more than we need to read or study. I have had much experience in this matter and know the difficulties in doing this. Many times while we are reading and studying the Word, it is

difficult to stop reading to pray. Thus, we must learn to read
while we pray and pray while we read. We must make our
reading our praying and our praying our reading. Eventually,
it will not matter whether we are reading or praying because
our reading and our praying will be mingled together. Also,
we do not need to pray in a formal way. We can simply read
and pray in a natural, spontaneous way. Instead of exercising
our mind, we should exercise our spirit.

RELEASING THE SPIRIT BY
REJOICING, PRAYING, THANKING, AND PRAISING

We not only must pray but also thank the Lord, praise
Him, and rejoice in Him. To do this is to open our mouth, our
"chimney." Instead of keeping the chimney closed and thereby
choking off the draft, we must open the chimney. When we
take the cover off the chimney by opening our mouth to
rejoice, we cause the Spirit to burn. Instead of reading the
Word in a formal way, we should remove the covers, open the
chimney, and let the air in by rejoicing while we read. Then
the fire will burn. At times we should even be beside ourselves when we read the Word. In 2 Corinthians 5:13 Paul
says, "For whether we were beside ourselves, it was to God; or
whether we are sober-minded, it is for you." Before man we
should be sober, but before God and in His presence we must
be beside ourselves. In other words, we must be released from
our self. If we have never been beside ourselves before God,
we are somewhat abnormal Christians. We need to release
ourselves by opening our mouth to rejoice and sing.

We must learn how to release the Spirit. This matter of
releasing the Spirit has much to do with rejoicing, praying,
thanking the Lord, and praising. In 1 Thessalonians 5:16-19
Paul says, "Always rejoice, unceasingly pray, in everything
give thanks; for this is the will of God in Christ Jesus for you.
Do not quench the Spirit." This short passage mentions four
matters: rejoicing, praying, giving thanks, and not quenching
the Spirit. It is clear from this passage that the matter of not
quenching the Spirit is very much related to the other three
matters of rejoicing, praying, and giving thanks. If we do not
rejoice, pray, or give thanks to the Lord, we will surely quench

the Spirit. Therefore, we must learn to rejoice, pray, thank, and praise so that the Spirit will not be quenched. This is very simple yet very vital.

Much of the time we choke off the draft and quench the Spirit because our spirit and mind remain closed. If we would simply open ourselves, the draft would come in, and the Holy Spirit would burn. The way to open our being is simple; it is to rejoice, pray, thank, and praise. Some might say that they do not have the grace to be open and that if they had the grace, they would be open. This is not right. We ourselves must open our being and let the air come in. If we allow the air to come in, the Spirit will burn in us.

OUR NEED TO BE SIMPLE AND OPEN

Today in Christianity there are two kinds of people. On the one hand, there are the worldly, backslidden believers who have no heart for the Lord. They are indifferent toward spiritual things, the things of the Lord, and come to the meetings in an indifferent way. Obviously, it is very difficult for such persons to open themselves. On the other hand, there are the so-called spiritual believers who are often so spiritual that they close themselves. Thus, both the backsliding believers and the spiritual believers close themselves so that there is no opening or entrance for the draft and, consequently, no burning of the Spirit in them.

We should not consider ourselves better than the backslidden believers. We should not think that although they have not seen a vision, we have. We should not think that we are so spiritual or consider ourselves higher than others. Instead, we should remove the cover from our being, allow the draft to come in, and let the Holy Spirit burn. We should be simple and open like a child (Matt. 18:3). For example, when we pray, we should not pray in an overly spiritual manner; rather, we should pray like a child (cf. Luke 18:10-14). Our urgent need as Christians who are seeking the Lord is that we open ourselves, make ourselves simple, and remove all the coverings so that the Spirit can get through and can burn within us.

BEING SIMPLE AND OPEN IN THE MEETINGS

The longer we meet together, the more formal we tend to become, and the more formal we become, the more we quench the Spirit. When we are formal in the meetings, everyone is careful not to open himself, and no one dares to open his mouth. We must break through this barrier, forget about everything, and make our meetings simple. We should come to the meeting as if we have just been saved. Inwardly we should be new. There should be nothing old; everything should be in newness.

Furthermore, we must take care of others in the meeting. All the children of God should come to the meeting and feel free to participate. When we pray too spiritually, we intimidate those who are uncomfortable to open their mouths and those who are afraid that they do not come up to our standard. Sometimes in the meetings the saints only say amen when the more spiritual brothers speak and never when the younger ones share. This shows that they prefer the spiritual ones. However, the spiritual ones do not need any more encouragement because they are already bold enough. The younger saints, on the other hand, are weak and timid and need our encouragement. When they pray, we should say amen to encourage them.

We should not make the meetings too spiritual because this kills the meeting. The more spiritual the brothers become, the more dead they become and the more dead the meetings become. We must forget about spirituality and be simple and open. We must endeavor not to know spirituality, Christianity, knowledge, doctrines, or anything else except to open ourselves, to be simple, to praise the Lord, and to remove the covers and let the draft in so that the Spirit can burn. In our meetings there must be a real burning. We should pray as children so that others will be encouraged to pray. If we were like children, our meetings would be simple, free, and open. Our meetings must liberate and release people, not bind them. Whenever people come to our meetings, they should have the sense that they have been liberated, set free, and released. For this we need the burning of the Spirit.

This matter is very much in the hands of the responsible and leading ones. Those who are taking the lead in the churches must take care of this responsibility. If they do not take care of these matters, the Spirit will always be quenched in the meetings. The responsible ones must take the lead to open themselves, to break through the barrier of formality, to forget about spiritual rules and regulations, and to even forget about spirituality. They must realize that we do not want anything other than Christ Himself in the Spirit. What we need today is not more knowledge but to be in the spirit. If we have the burning of the Holy Spirit within us, we will have power, impact, and authority. Thus, by the Lord's mercy, grace, and help, let us determine to learn to open ourselves and to let the draft in so that the Spirit may burn within us.

A FEW MATTERS THAT CAN QUENCH THE SPIRIT

Spiritually speaking, it is relatively easy to start the fire, but it is just as easy to quench the fire. Even a small matter such as being a little careless or saying something slightly improper can quench the fire of the Spirit. When you want to start a fire in a stove, you must do certain things to help the fire to burn. In the same way, the Spirit needs our cooperation in certain matters in order to burn. Otherwise, it is difficult for the Spirit to burn. If we are loose and careless in our speaking, in our attitude, and in doing things, no matter how small they may seem, we will quench the Spirit. Thus, we must be careful not to be careless or loose.

Many times in the meetings and in our daily life we have the sense to pray, but we do not obey this sense. Even a little disobedience like this can quench the Spirit. However, if we obey this feeling and pray, the Spirit will burn. If you are a sister in the kitchen washing the dishes, and you have a feeling to pray, then you should immediately pray. There is no need to stop washing; you can pray as you wash. However, if you have the burden to stop washing and pray, you may stop and kneel down in the kitchen to pray. There is no need to go anywhere else to pray.

Gossip also quenches the Spirit. Nothing quenches the Spirit so much as a little gossip. We must realize that whenever we gossip with others, we are quenching the Spirit. As Christians we must completely give up our gossiping. We may think that these matters are trivial and do not matter. However, they do matter because they determine whether the Spirit will burn or whether it will be quenched. If we turn our gossip into prayer, the Spirit will burn. Joking can also kill the Spirit. If we joke too much, we will quench the Spirit. This does not mean that we must always be formal or official. However, we should not joke because our joking does not help the Spirit to burn but only quenches it.

When we go to the Lord to pray, we should not consider and think about what to pray, because this also quenches the Spirit. When we go to pray, we should forget about everything and pray in a spontaneous, natural, and living way. The more we pray in this way, the more we will have the flow and the burning of the Spirit. We must take care of all these small matters because these are the things that can quench the Spirit. If we take care of these matters, we will be those who are always on fire. The basic matter is that we must learn how to open ourselves by rejoicing, praying unceasingly, and giving thanks in everything.

CHAPTER FOUR

EXERCISING OUR SPIRIT TO EXPRESS GOD

Scripture Reading: Eph. 4:6; 5:18b-20

GOD'S RELATIONSHIP WITH MAN

Ephesians 4:6 says, "One God and Father of all, who is over all and through all and in all." Although the phrases "over all," "through all," and "in all" are very brief and simple, the secret and mystery of God's relationship with man is contained in them. God is not only over us but also through us and in us in order to be expressed, manifested, glorified, and exhibited. We must realize that these three phrases are in a particular order. Everyone who has considered God and believes that there is a God knows that this God is over the people on the earth. There is no doubt that God is over all of us. However, not many have considered that God is through us and is doing something through us. Furthermore, we who are Christians know and experience God being in us. To us, God is not only over us and through us, but even more, He is in us and is abiding in us, dwelling in us, and mingling Himself with us for His expression, manifestation, exhibition, and glorification. We were made for God and made to fulfill His purpose, which is that we would contain Him and express Him (Rom. 9:21, 23; Gen. 1:26).

We need to read the Scriptures in the light of God's purpose, which is that God would express Himself through humanity. Then we will realize that although God is the invisible and hidden God, a God who always hides Himself (1 Tim. 1:17; Isa. 45:15), He also has the desire to manifest and express Himself through man. God can only be seen through humanity. This is proved by John 1:18, which says, "No one has ever seen

God; the only begotten Son, who is in the bosom of the Father, He has declared Him." God does not express Himself through Himself or in Himself. He only expresses Himself through man and in man. Although I do not know why God desires this, I do know that this is the desire of His heart.

To illustrate this matter, consider a light bulb. The sole purpose of a light bulb is to give light. It has no other purpose. If a light bulb is not attached to an electrical socket so that it can express the light, it is meaningless and good for nothing because it was specifically made for the purpose of receiving and expressing light. Furthermore, electricity cannot be expressed by itself. In order to be expressed, it needs a light bulb that has been made purposely to express electricity. Similarly, God would never express Himself by Himself. He needs some "bulbs," people who were made for the purpose of expressing Him. We must realize that we have been made for this purpose. We are vessels and containers that are good for nothing but to receive, contain, and express God. As human beings, we must know what we are and what we are good for. We may realize that as Christians we are the saints, the believers, and even the Lord's servants and His children. However, we may have never had the thought that we are containers and vessels of God and that we were made specifically for the purpose of containing and expressing God, just as light bulbs are made specifically to contain and express light. We must realize that God is over us, through us, and in us and that He is dwelling in us, abiding in us, and remaining in us. Thus, we must be the containers to contain and express Him.

USING OUR SPIRIT TO SUBSTANTIATE GOD

We must also realize that the only way we as containers can express God is by exercising and releasing our spirit, because today God is Spirit, and this divine Spirit is in our human spirit (John 4:24; Rom. 8:16; 2 Tim. 4:22). Many Christians who have been saved, redeemed, and regenerated do not realize that they have a human spirit. Some believe that the spirit and the soul are synonymous, and others say that the spirit is the same thing as the heart. However, if we are going to realize the spiritual things and understand the secret and mystery of

God, we must realize that we have a spirit (Job 32:8; Zech. 12:1). It would be impossible for us to physically grow if we did not realize that we have a stomach and thus never exercised or used our stomach. In order to grow, we must use and exercise our stomach every day to take food in and digest it. God purposely created us with a stomach so that we could take food in for our growth. In the same principle, there is an organ within us called the human spirit which God created for the purpose of receiving Him.

Our physical body is very complicated and is composed of many different organs. In particular, we have specific organs which give us the five senses of sight, hearing, smell, taste, and touch. These organs are our eyes, ears, nose, mouth, and body. If you are in a meeting and try to use your eyes to listen to the message, you will not believe that there is someone speaking because you are using the wrong organ to substantiate the speaking. If someone is showing you different colored objects, and you are trying to "hear" the colors with your ears, you will not believe in those colors because you are using the wrong organ. If there is an odor in the room, and your nose is not functioning because you have a cold, you will not sense the odor. You cannot see, touch, or hear the odor; only your nose can sense the odor.

Thus, the principle is that in order to substantiate a certain thing, you need the proper organ with which to substantiate it. You cannot substantiate color using the ear or substantiate sound using the tongue. In the same way, God is Spirit; He is a spiritual substance. He is so real, yet if we do not use the right organ to substantiate Him, He will not be real to us. Since God is a spiritual substance, we must substantiate Him with a spiritual organ—our human spirit.

God created us with ears so that we could substantiate sound, and He created us with eyes so that we could substantiate the visible things. Even more, God created us with a spirit (Zech. 12:1; Prov. 20:27). Thus, besides the five senses of our physical body, we have a spiritual sense, the sense of our spirit. Our spirit is not the same as our heart or our mind. Our spirit is the organ by which we sense, receive, contain, and express God. Once we realize that we have a human spirit, we can locate God because today God is in our spirit. On the one hand, Christ has ascended and been exalted to the heavens, but on the other hand, Christ the Lord as the Spirit is in our spirit (Rom. 8:16; 2 Tim. 4:22).

RELEASING OUR SPIRIT

The way we can express and manifest God is by opening and releasing our spirit. If we release our spirit, the very God who is in our spirit will automatically be released because He has committed Himself to our spirit. To illustrate, suppose I put a key in a brother's hand. If the brother closes his hand and never opens it, the hand becomes a prison to the key, and the key cannot be released. As long as he holds the key fast, no one can see the key, and the key cannot be released. However, once he simply opens his hand, the key is released. There is no need for him to exercise his arms, legs, feet, head, or any other part of his body. All he must do is open his hand, and the key will be released.

In a similar way, God today is in our spirit, but most of the time our spirit remains closed while our mind and mouth are open. When we come together to meet, we may know how to exercise our mouth, but we do not know how to exercise our spirit. Consequently, our mouths are open and active to gossip and talk about other people, but our spirit is closed. Then when someone suggests that we pray, everyone closes his mouth. The reason for this is simply that we do not know how to exercise our spirit. If we were those living in the Lord and walking in His presence, we would shut our mouths if we heard someone gossiping or speaking vain things. Furthermore, if given the opportunity to glorify, exalt, and express the Lord, we would pray, sing a hymn, and release our spirit.

EXERCISING OUR SPIRIT BY SINGING

My only burden is that the Lord would impress us that as Christians who are seeking the Lord, we must realize the secret and mystery of our relationship with the Lord, which is the matter of the exercise of our spirit. We must open our spirit, exercise it, and use it. The most helpful way to exercise our spirit is to pray, but sometimes it is even better to sing.

We may sing something short such as a chorus in a loud way, or we may sing something long such as a psalm in a quiet way. Ephesians 5:19 and Colossians 3:16 both mention psalms, hymns, and spiritual songs. In terms of length, psalms are the longest, hymns are shorter, and spiritual songs, which are like the choruses of hymns, are the shortest. Many times in the meetings we should sing a short chorus with our spirit and from our spirit.

We should each have some choruses memorized so that we can sing them all the time in our spirit and with our spirit. When the young people want to exercise, they often play basketball, baseball, or football. That is the best way for them to exercise their body. However, in order to play, they need a ball. Similarly, the best way for us to exercise our spirit is to sing, but we need a "ball." We need to have some choruses in us so that we can sing them all the time. Then we must exercise to sing, not merely from our mouth but from our spirit and in our spirit.

Recently we have been working to prepare a hymnal. If the Lord is willing, it would be good if He raised up some saints to compose some songs on the book of Ephesians, perhaps a song for each chapter. Then when the saints come together, they could use these songs to sing the whole book of Ephesians. In addition, it would be wonderful to have songs on Romans 8 and Colossians 1. Many Christians today sing the Old Testament psalms, but that is not up to the standard of the New Testament. Very few people have composed songs on the New Testament revelation.

We must learn to sing because the more we sing, the more we get out of our mind and forget about our circumstances. The more we sing, the more we are in the spirit and the more our spirit is open and released. This is not my thought or opinion; this is the thought of the Holy Spirit and the thought of the apostle Paul. In Ephesians 5:18-19, Paul says that we should be filled in spirit, speaking to one another by singing. If we speak to one another by singing a psalm, hymn, or spiritual song, our spirits will be exercised and the Spirit will come out. We should not try to sing in a musical way but in a spiritual way. We should even forget about the music, the

meter, and the rhyme. I am not a musician or an expert
singer; I cannot sing that well. However, whether I sing well
or not, I must sing. We must learn how to praise the Lord by
singing. We need to read, study, and be able to recite some
hymns. This way we can sing on the street or in the car. This
matter is revealed not only in the New Testament but also in
the Old Testament. When the people of Israel came together
to worship God in the Old Testament, they sang as they were
on their way to Zion (Psa. 133:1-3). If we sing while we are
coming to the meeting in the car, the meeting will be in the
heavens. We must learn to exercise and open our spirit by
singing.

FULFILLING THE LORD'S WILL
BY EXERCISING OUR SPIRIT

We must realize that God's intention and purpose for us is
not that we would do something for Him but that we would be
a vessel to contain and express Him. As long as we contain
and express God, we will be in a proper condition. Today
many Christians are talking about overcoming and being
victorious over sin. However, we will never overcome sin by
focusing on victory over sin. If we forget about sin and instead
sing and praise all the time, we will be in the heavens, sin will
not be able to touch us, and we will have the victory over sin.
Many people are seeking to know the Lord's mind and will.
However, if we would sing, the Lord's will would be clear to us
in our spirit. The right way for a Christian to take is to exercise the spirit, contact God, receive the Lord, and express
Him. If we have this, we will have everything, including
victory over the world, sin, and the self.

The Lord's purpose is that we would express Him. Let us
forget everything else and simply learn how to exercise our
spirit by praying, praising, and singing. If we do this, the
Spirit, who is the Lord Himself, will automatically be released
from our spirit. Then we will grow every day and will be
transformed by the renewing of our mind (Rom. 12:2). It is
not by teaching, doctrine, or knowledge that we grow but by
the exercise of the spirit. Thus, we must learn how to exercise
our spirit so that we may continually grow and experience,

enjoy, and partake of Christ. If we do this, we will be in Him all the time. This is the meaning of abiding in the Lord. This message is not a teaching or a doctrine. Rather, it is like a map to show us the way to drive. If we do not actually drive, the map is of no use, but if we begin to drive, this map will be very useful. We must learn to exercise our spirit by praying, praising, and singing.

ABOUT THE AUTHOR

Witness Lee was born in 1905 in northern China and raised in a Christian family. At age 19 he was fully captured for Christ and immediately consecrated himself to preach the gospel for the rest of his life. Early in his service, he met Watchman Nee, a renowned preacher, teacher, and writer. Witness Lee labored together with Watchman Nee under his direction. In 1934 Watchman Nee entrusted Witness Lee with the responsibility for his publication operation, called the Shanghai Gospel Bookroom.

Prior to the Communist takeover in 1949, Witness Lee was sent by Watchman Nee and his other co-workers to Taiwan to ensure that the things delivered to them by the Lord would not be lost. Watchman Nee instructed Witness Lee to continue the former's publishing operation abroad as the Taiwan Gospel Bookroom, which has been publicly recognized as the publisher of Watchman Nee's works outside China. Witness Lee's work in Taiwan manifested the Lord's abundant blessing. From a mere 350 believers, newly fled from the mainland, the churches in Taiwan grew to 20,000 in five years.

In 1962 Witness Lee felt led of the Lord to come to the United States, settling in California. During his 35 years of service in the U.S., he ministered in weekly meetings and weekend conferences, delivering several thousand spoken messages. Much of his speaking has since been published as over 400 titles. Many of these have been translated into over fourteen languages. He gave his last public conference in February 1997 at the age of 91.

He leaves behind a prolific presentation of the truth in the Bible. His major work, *Life-study of the Bible,* comprises over 25,000 pages of commentary on every book of the Bible from the perspective of the believers' enjoyment and experience of God's divine life in Christ through the Holy Spirit. Witness Lee was the chief editor of a new translation of the New Testament into Chinese called the Recovery Version and directed the translation of the same into English. The Recovery Version also appears in a number of other languages. He provided an extensive body of footnotes, outlines, and spiritual cross references. A radio broadcast of his messages can be heard on Christian radio stations in the United States. In 1965 Witness Lee founded Living Stream Ministry, a non-profit corporation, located in Anaheim, California, which officially presents his and Watchman Nee's ministry.

Witness Lee's ministry emphasizes the experience of Christ as life and the practical oneness of the believers as the Body of Christ. Stressing the importance of attending to both these matters, he led the churches under his care to grow in Christian life and function. He was unbending in his conviction that God's goal is not narrow sectarianism but the Body of Christ. In time, believers began to meet simply as the church in their localities in response to this conviction. In recent years a number of new churches have been raised up in Russia and in many eastern European countries.

OTHER BOOKS PUBLISHED BY
Living Stream Ministry

Titles by Witness Lee:

Abraham—Called by God	0-7363-0359-6
The Experience of Life	0-87083-417-7
The Knowledge of Life	0-87083-419-3
The Tree of Life	0-87083-300-6
The Economy of God	0-87083-415-0
The Divine Economy	0-87083-268-9
God's New Testament Economy	0-87083-199-2
The World Situation and God's Move	0-87083-092-9
Christ vs. Religion	0-87083-010-4
The All-inclusive Christ	0-87083-020-1
Gospel Outlines	0-87083-039-2
Character	0-87083-322-7
The Secret of Experiencing Christ	0-87083-227-1
The Life and Way for the Practice of the Church Life	0-87083-785-0
The Basic Revelation in the Holy Scriptures	0-87083-105-4
The Crucial Revelation of Life in the Scriptures	0-87083-372-3
The Spirit with Our Spirit	0-87083-798-2
Christ as the Reality	0-87083-047-3
The Central Line of the Divine Revelation	0-87083-960-8
The Full Knowledge of the Word of God	0-87083-289-1
Watchman Nee—A Seer of the Divine Revelation ...	0-87083-625-0

Titles by Watchman Nee:

How to Study the Bible	0-7363-0407-X
God's Overcomers	0-7363-0433-9
The New Covenant	0-7363-0088-0
The Spiritual Man 3 volumes	0-7363-0269-7
Authority and Submission	0-7363-0185-2
The Overcoming Life	1-57593-817-0
The Glorious Church	0-87083-745-1
The Prayer Ministry of the Church	0-87083-860-1
The Breaking of the Outer Man and the Release ...	1-57593-955-X
The Mystery of Christ	1-57593-954-1
The God of Abraham, Isaac, and Jacob	0-87083-932-2
The Song of Songs	0-87083-872-5
The Gospel of God 2 volumes	1-57593-953-3
The Normal Christian Church Life	0-87083-027-9
The Character of the Lord's Worker	1-57593-322-5
The Normal Christian Faith	0-87083-748-6
Watchman Nee's Testimony	0-87083-051-1

Available at
Christian bookstores, or contact Living Stream Ministry
2431 W. La Palma Ave. • Anaheim, CA 92801
1-800-549-5164 • www.livingstream.com